The Gift of
THE HOLY GHOST

Written and Illustrated
by
Phyllis Carol Olive

Published and Distributed by:

Granite Publishing and Distribution, LLC
868 North 1430 West
Orem, Utah 84057
(801) 229-9023 • Toll Free (800) 574-5779
Fax (801) 229-1924

Clip Art from Corel Corporation

Library of Congress Catalog Card Number: 2003104941
ISBN: 1-932280-08-1

Printed in Korea

10 9 8 7 6 5 4 3 2 1

*H*eavenly Father is the great God of heaven. Our brother Jesus is also a God and so is the Holy Ghost. These three gods make up what we call the Godhead.

Jesus and Heavenly Father have bodies of flesh and bones like you and me, but the Holy Ghost is different. He is still a spirit person. All three of them love us very much.

Long before we were born we lived with Heavenly Father as his spirit children. One day he called a Grand Council of all his children. He told us of his plan to send us away to earth school where we could learn about good and evil and where we would receive a mortal body. It was a good plan. We were so happy that we all shouted for joy.

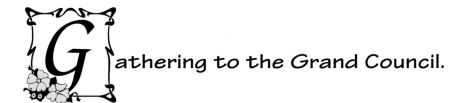 athering to the Grand Council.

*H*eavenly Father told Jesus to make an earth for us to live on while we were away. Since we would miss him very much, Father told us we can always talk to him through prayer.

ur earthly home.

*H*eavenly Father told us that we will be tested while we live on earth to see if we will be good or bad. He told us that only those who choose to be good will be able to live with him when our earth school is over. Because he wants us all to live with him again, he gave us two very special gifts—

he Light of his Son Jesus Christ, and the gift of the Holy Ghost.

The Light of Christ is given to every spirit child that leaves heaven to come to earth.

The Light of Christ will teach us right from wrong and act as our conscience as long as we live.

If we listen to our conscience, it will help us choose the right and will help us be worthy to return to Heavenly Father when our earth life is over.

 ow, the devil does not want us to return to Heavenly Father. He wants us to do bad things and break the commandments.

If we listen to our conscience, or the Light of Christ, it will help us know right from wrong and will help us choose the right each and every time.

The second gift that God gives us is the gift of the Holy Ghost. It is given to us only after we are made clean in the waters of baptism.

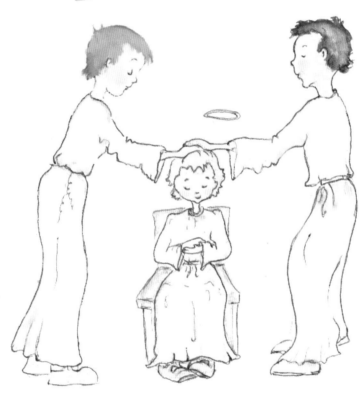

Men with the Priesthood will then lay their hands upon our heads and confirm us members of The Church of Jesus Christ of Latter-day Saints.

They will then give us one of the greatest gifts God can give his children by saying, "Receive the Holy Ghost."

*T*he gift of the Holy Ghost will help us in many ways.

The most important assignment Heavenly Father has given the Holy Ghost is to testify of him and of his Son Jesus Christ that they live and love us. Even though we may not see Heavenly Father right now, he misses us very much and wants us always to remember him. He also wants us to remember his Son Jesus Christ and all that he has done for us.

The Holy Ghost testifies of Heavenly Father and Jesus.

*H*eavenly Father has given the Holy Ghost other assignments as well.

He is a great teacher and will help us learn things. He will even help us remember things we might have forgotten.

*T*he Holy Ghost will fill our minds with knowledge and give us understanding and help us to be wise in everything we do if we listen to his still, small voice.

If we learn to listen to his promptings he will teach us many things.

The Holy Ghost is also a comforter. Sometimes when bad things happen to us he helps us feel better.

He helps us understand that when people or animals we love die, they go to heaven where they will be happy forever and ever. Even dead fish go to heaven. It is a wonderful place, a place where people and even little fish are smiling and happy.

eavenly Father must love us very much to give us such a wonderful gift as the Holy Ghost. It is up to us to keep this gift. If we sin or do mean things the Holy Ghost will leave us.

20

If we lose the Holy Ghost we must repent and ask for God's forgiveness. Only after we have made it right can the Holy Ghost return to us again and continue to help us.

Great rewards await us if we listen to the promptings of the Holy Spirit. If we do so and obey all of God's commandments we will be worthy to return to Heavenly Father when our earth school is over, and we will be happy in his heavenly kingdom forever.

We must always try to be worthy of the Holy Ghost and stay true to the Light of Christ. They will both help us return to Heavenly Father and live with our eternal family in the Celestial Kingdom of God.